INTELLECTUAL PROPERTY DIY™

INTELLECTUAL PROPERTY DIY™

TRADEMARKS

FILE YOUR OWN IP APPLICATION
EFFICIENTLY, WITHOUT A LAWYER

T. R. MARLOWE

This book makes reference to copyrighted material found at USPTO.gov, by the United States Patent and Trademark Office.

This book may not be duplicated, copied, reprinted, manufactured, stored, or sold without direct permission of the publisher.

© 2024 IPDIY

Published in the United States by IPDIY, an imprint and division of Filling A Void Enterprises
Topeka, Kansas
All Rights Reserved

ISBN: 979-8-9898343-3-4

Library of Congress Control Number: 2024901921

Dedication

First, giving honor, praise and thanks to God, for all the many ways he has blessed my life. With this book, and others to come, my ultimate goal is to make a positive impact, in the lives of others. This book is dedicated to my parents, who TAUGHT me how to use my gifts, by first SHOWING me how to give.

In loving memory of my dad.

To the teachers that saw something special in this kid, to those that encouraged me, cheered and supported me through the years, to those who could never find the words to just say "good job", and lastly, to my heartbeats...

Em, X, J, and Ry, this one's for you.

Disclaimer

I AM NOT A LAWYER, NOR AM I GIVING LEGAL ADVICE.

This book, *Intellectual Property DIY*™ Trademarks, is not designed to teach law. The *IP Planner & Punch List*™ will assist in keeping your details organized, as you prepare to file your IP application, and beyond.

Always consult a lawyer, if you can afford one. This book was birthed out of my love for sharing information. After taking a course to learn how to write a patent, I began looking at the other forms of intellectual property (IP) courses that were being offered. I discovered that the USPTO has tools and resources that enable you to file your own IP application, without hiring a lawyer. After completing an 8-course certification in Intellectual Property, I knew it was time to document my findings. I will act as your "project manager", as you learn to DIY.

Is this for everyone? No!

Please note, this will take some reading and understanding, on your end. The USPTO has also provided a series of videos to help you grasp the subjects and terms. (At the time of creating this book, some of those videos were being updated, due to an update to the "search" site). As "project manager", I'll point you to where to find the answers to your questions, directly from the USPTO. When it's time to fill out the application, you've done the research, you'll already know what information is being requested, AND you'll move through the application more efficiently.

This book does not promise any type of degree, registration, certification, level of learning or understanding, or any other achievement. This book is solely designed to point to resources which can assist the user in securing their IP.

TABLE OF CONTENTS

DISCLAIMER *(please read)* — vi

I. <u>INTRODUCTION</u>
   Purpose — 1
   Interactive *pages*

II. <u>FIRST THINGS FIRST</u>
   Create *A User ID (IMPORTANT)* — 2
   IP PUNCH LIST ™ *The Resources* — 3
    • *Trademark Assistance Center (phone/email)*
    • *Trademark Basics Registration Toolkit (Review @ USPTO.gov)*
    • *Trademark Basics Bootcamp (LIVE virtual presentation - USPTO.gov)*
    • *USPTO tutorial videos*
   Terms *You'll Want To Know* — 4
   Trademark *Word Search* — 5

III. <u>PREP WORK</u>
   Why *You Should Do It* **-** *(See Trademark Basics Registration Toolkit @ USPTO.gov)* — 6
   Watch *USPTO Tutorial Videos (Use note paper included)* — 7

TABLE OF CONTENTS

III. PREP WORK (CONTINUED)

IP PUNCH LIST™ - Sketch a design or logo (if needed) — 17

IP PUNCH LIST™ - The Search — 18

Brainstorm exercise (Do **BEFORE** search) — 19
• Selecting your word mark

Search (by USPTO recommendation) — 20

Brainstorm exercise (Do **AFTER** search) — 21
• Class of Goods & Services WorkUp

BEFORE YOU BEGIN the trademark application — 22

IP PLANNER™ Card — 23

CHALLENGE Questions — 24

Trademark Crossword Puzzle — 25

IV. APPLICATION PROCESS

IP PUNCH LIST™ - The Application — 26
(Reminder - Refer to "TEAS Nuts & Bolts" videos to help with application)

IP PLANNER™ Log Sheet — 27

TABLE OF CONTENTS

V. FOLLOW-UP

    Office Actions   32

    Maintenance   33

VI. EXTRA FORMS (5 SETS)   34

VII. REFERENCE   90

INTRODUCTION

PURPOSE

This book will point to resources that assist in learning how to file an intellectual property (IP) application efficiently, without a lawyer. Make sure you have read the disclaimer at the front of the book.

INTERACTIVE PAGES

This collection of organizational tools, in the form of planner sheets and checklists, were created to assist in the "prep work", for filing a trademark application. NONE of these activity pages are required, in order to file a trademark application. The planner pages will give the user a place to brainstorm, while gathering details, as information is learned from the USPTO.gov website.

IP Planner™- These forms will assist in organizing IP application information and allow for record keeping. **The IP Planners do not have to be completed, in order to file an IP application.**

Punch List™- These checklists are designed to assist in learning key terms and subjects. The checklists are to be used along with official information from USPTO.gov. Check the "box" to know you have reviewed the subject. **The Punch List does not have to be completed, in order to file an IP application.**

Puzzle Games - These puzzles assist in learning key words and subjects. **Puzzles are not required to file an IP application.**

CREATE A USER ID

STEP 1

GO TO USPTO.GOV

People think I'm joking with this. **THIS IS STEP 1.** If you're serious about learning how to file your own IP application, you will need login credentials. I suggest you do this now, so that when you're researching the USPTO site and it randomly asks you to log in, you won't have to stop and try to navigate through that.

You'll thank me later.

Here's the steps:
1. Go to USPTO.gov
2. At the top of the page, click MENU
3. Scroll down to MyUSPTO. Click that.
4. On this page, you can create an account. If you already have an account, you can sign in here.

FIRST THINGS FIRST   Intellectual Property DIY Trademarks

IP PUNCH LIST™

FIRST THINGS FIRST – THE RESOURCES

TRADEMARK ASSISTANCE CENTER

You're not alone in this. If you get stuck, reach out to the USPTO by phone or email. However, they WILL NOT give legal advice.

- ☐ USPTO.gov
  Menu ==> Trademarks => More Trademarks ==> Contact Trademarks
- ☐ Phone: 1-800-786-9199
- ☐ TrademarkAssistanceCenter@uspto.gov

TRADEMARK BASICS REGISTRATION TOOLKIT

START HERE! This document is FULL of information to assist you in the learning phase.

- ☐ What is a trademark
- ☐ Put public on notice
- ☐ Trademark symbols
- ☐ Trademark process
- ☐ Do I need an attorney?
- ☐ Conduct a search
- ☐ Application process
- ☐ Maintenance   *and more...*

Menu ==> Trademarks ==> Getting Started ==> Trademark Basics (scroll down)

TRADEMARK BASICS BOOT CAMP

More resources at USPTO.gov

LIVE presentations - 8 modules

- ☐ Fundamentals
- ☐ Registration process
- ☐ Searching
- ☐ Application
- ☐ Application filing
- ☐ Responding to office action
- ☐ Maintenance
- ☐ Q & A panel   *and more...*

Menu ==> Trademarks ==> Getting Started ==> Trademark Basics (scroll down)

VIDEOS - TEAS NUTS & BOLTS

Due to an update to the "search" system (11/23), some USPTO tutorial videos were removed and are being updated, at the time of printing this book. Review available videos BEFORE and DURING application process.

- ☐ TEAS Plus vs TEAS Standard
- ☐ Applicant Information
- ☐ Mark Drawing Page
- ☐ Additional Statements
- ☐ G & S TEAS Plus
- ☐ G & S TEAS Standard
- ☐ Filing Basis
- ☐ Correspondence Informaton
- ☐ Signature Information
- ☐ Validation Page

MENU ==> Trademarks ==> Application process ==> Apply online ==> Scroll down to Nuts & Bolts videos

and more...

Terms You'll Want To Know

(USPTO videos/website will cover these terms)

1(a)	Registration #
1(b)	®
Disclaimer	Serial #
Domicile address	Services
Drawing page	Service mark
	Specimen
Filing basis	SM
Filing fee	
First use anywhere	TAC
First use in commerce	TEAS plus
Goods	TEAS standard
	TM
Intellectual Property (IP)	Trademark
	Trademark ID Manual
International Class ID Manual	Trademark/ Service mark Appl.
Legal entity	United States Patent and Trademark Office (USPTO)
Liklihood of confusion	
Maintenance fee	Validation page
Mark	
Office action	Word mark
Owner address	
Owner of mark	

TRADEMARK WORD SEARCH

Find and circle trademark related words

L	R	U	S	T	I	M	M	S	E	R	V	I	C	E	M	A	R	K	C
E	M	M	U	N	I	C	A	T	I	C	N	O	X	Y	H	G	E	7	U
G	T	I	L	I	B	9	T	A	P	L	O	C	R	E	Y	T	I	T	I
A	R	E	F	I	L	I	N	G	B	A	S	I	S	R	J	F	O	E	T
L	O	R	P	M	O	C	I	M	A	S	N	I	E	L	J	I	E	A	A
E	F	3	T	S	E	N	O	H	R	S	7	D	R	H	N	O	M	S	Y
N	A	C	U	S	T	S	U	E	P	O	R	T	V	P	E	F	R	P	S
T	X	P	I	Y	E	P	M	M	R	E	V	O	I	M	A	F	T	L	E
I	A	T	R	A	D	E	M	A	R	K	K	F	C	E	N	I	O	U	1
T	V	A	R	T	N	C	R	R	E	K	O	T	E	A	T	C	M	S	A
Y	I	T	A	C	T	I	T	I	M	M	R	T	S	A	R	E	T	I	M
P	E	C	R	E	P	M	E	R	D	N	Y	2	R	F	S	A	O	R	S
A	R	R	O	M	M	E	T	N	M	M	L	O	C	N	I	C	A	M	E
T	E	I	T	N	E	N	M	I	A	M	E	C	I	I	M	T	T	N	A
D	I	S	C	L	A	I	M	E	R	P	E	R	P	O	C	I	M	U	R
B	M	S	C	S	S	E	N	O	K	Y	T	I	L	A	P	O	R	T	C
I	S	S	C	A	R	T	S	E	M	O	G	O	O	D	S	N	O	D	H

CLASS	DISCLAIMER	FILING BASIS
GOODS	LEGAL ENTITY	MARK
OFFICE ACTION	SEARCH	SERVICE MARK
SERVICES	SPECIMEN	TAC
TEAS PLUS	TRADEMARK	1A

PREP WORK
Why You Should Do It

Doing the "prep work" will help you move through the online application system more efficiently. I can already hear critics saying, "All this is NOT necessary". This book is NOT for them. Keep going...

The USPTO provides a manual called, Trademark Basics Registration Toolkit. **THIS IS SOMETHING YOU WANT TO REVIEW.** The USPTO is updating the, over 34+ videos that were once available on their website. Check back periodically for updated videos. In the meantime, click on hyperlinks on USPTO.gov, as they are full of information and may go into further details on a subject. **(For example: Menu ==> Trademarks ==> Getting Started ==> Trademark Basics (click links).** Take time to browse the website. The answers to your questions are there. The pages of this book are ordered intentionally.

STAY THE COURSE...

At the time of printing this book, the "TEAS Nuts & Bolts" videos are available. Watch these videos now AND refer back to them, as you move through the trademark application. Use provided note paper.

PREP WORK Intellectual Property DIY Trademarks
NOTES

Video title _____

Intellectual Property DIY Trademarks   PREP WORK

NOTES

Video title _____

PREP WORK Intellectual Property DIY Trademarks

NOTES

Video title _____

Intellectual Property DIY Trademarks — PREP WORK

NOTES

Video title _____

PREP WORK

NOTES

Video title _____

Intellectual Property DIY Trademarks   PREP WORK

NOTES

Video title _____

PREP WORK　　　　　　　　　　　　　　Intellectual Property DIY Trademarks
NOTES

Video title _____

Intellectual Property DIY Trademarks PREP WORK

NOTES

Video title _____

PREP WORK   Intellectual Property DIY Trademarks

NOTES

Video title _____

Intellectual Property DIY Trademarks · PREP WORK

NOTES

Video title _____

PREP WORK Intellectual Property DIY Trademarks

IP PUNCH LIST™

SKETCH A LOGO OR DESIGN

Intellectual Property DIY Trademarks — PREP WORK

IP PUNCH LIST ™

PREP WORK – THE SEARCH

- ☐ *Watch USPTO tutorials

- ☐ Do a BRAINSTORM exercise (see worksheet) to come up with 1-5 ideas for a mark, in case your idea is already registered.

Videos/FAQ's on searching
Menu ==>
Trademarks ==>
Application Proc. =>
Search Our Trademark Database

- ☐ An attorney would do an extensive SEARCH. The USPTO gives YOU guidance on how to search BEFORE you apply for your mark.

- ☐ SEARCH for mark being used in commerce (as per USPTO). Use included note paper.
  - search USPTO site
  - search on social media
  - search on Google
  - search on internet

- ☐ Do a BRAINSTORM exercise (see worksheet) to determine the International Class(es) in which you want to file your mark. ==> There is a FEE per CLASS. Must select at least 1 class

- ☐ Filing basis?
  - 1(a)
  - 1(b)
  - Other (per USPTO)

- ☐ Prep your specimen

*In November 2023, the USPTO updated to a new SEARCH system. At the time of printing this book, the "TEAS Nuts and Bolts" videos were available.

PREP WORK   Intellectual Property DIY Trademarks

Brainstorm Exercise

You may already know what word(s) you want to file for a trademark. What if the word(s), slogan, etc. is already registered? Brainstorm 1-5 new options, as you prepare to SEARCH, according to USPTO recommendations.

☐ **WORD MARK, PHRASE, ETC.**

☐ **WORD MARK, PHRASE, ETC.**

☐ **WORD MARK, PHRASE, ETC.**

☐ **WORD MARK, PHRASE, ETC.**

☐ **WORD MARK, PHRASE, ETC.**

Intellectual Property DIY Trademarks   PREP WORK

SEARCH NOTES

PREP WORK   Intellectual Property DIY Trademarks

Brainstorm Exercise

Use this worksheet to plan which International Class(es) you want to file your mark under. **There is a FEE** for each class. You must choose at least 1 of the 45 classes. Refer to the TEAS Nuts & Bolts Goods & Services video that explains the ID manual. Remember: IN USE or INTENDED USE

List goods/services IN USE or INTENDED USE
ex. socks, hoodies, combs, brushes

☐ [   ]

List CLASS for each good/service
ex. 25, 21

☐ [   ]

Notes

☐ [   ]

Intellectual Property DIY Trademarks — PREP WORK

BEFORE YOU BEGIN
The Trademark Application

Please read all of this.

If you reached this point, you've been doing your work. Congratulations. By now, you have reviewed the Trademark Basic Registration Toolkit, you've watched available videos on the USPTO.gov web page, you sketched out a potential logo or design that maybe you'll have generated, you've done your brainstorming for the words you'll file for, you've done your searches, and you figured out what class(es) of goods or services you'll list in your application, by using the ID manual.

Whew, that's a lot!!! Just think how much you've learned. I was overwhelmed, the first time I completed a trademark application. I was all over the place. I didn't have good direction, but if you really did the prep work, NOW you have put yourself in a position to *efficiently* move through the application. This is not about going "fast", but you MAY move thru the next application quicker.

I created the **IP PLANNER**™ card so you can transfer all your brainstormed data, to one place. A clean slate, if you will, including name of the mark, class of goods OR services, (you may be filing for multiple classes), and the line items you want to use from the ID manual that describe how your mark is used, or will be used in commerce. Lastly, when you reach the VALIDATION page on the application, VERIFY what you have input, BEFORE you hit submit. Take your time, as the USPTO does not give refunds.

REMEMBER: IF YOU HAVE QUESTIONS, ASK THE HELP DESK OR SEEK OTHER HELP PROVIDED BY THE USPTO.

PREP WORK Intellectual Property DIY Trademarks

Word Mark	IP PLANNER™ CARD

	Filing basis

List goods/services

Date First Use Anywhere: Date First Use In Commerce:	Class(es)

Word Mark	IP PLANNER™ CARD

	Filing basis

List goods/services

Date First Use Anywhere: Date First Use In Commerce:	Class(es)

CHALLENGE QUESTIONS
(Did you find these answers in your research, on USPTO.gov?)

Do I have common law rights, even if I never file a trademark application?

Can I file one application, if the wordmark is a part of the logo, or do I need two separate applications?

If I originally file an application with a 1(b) filing basis, what are the additional fees to file a 1(a) filing basis?

Can I use the ™ sign before I file an application?

Are refunds available if I made a mistake?

There are 45 classes in the International Class ID Manual. Can multiple businesses share the same name, but in different classes?
• Goods are class 1 thru _____.
• Services are class _____ thru 45.

I got a letter from a business, stating that I owe money to keep my trademark active. Is this SPAM?

PREP WORK   Intellectual Property DIY Trademarks

TRADEMARK CROSSWORD PUZZLE

ACROSS
1. Similarity could cause rejection
4. Idea of self monitoring activity
5. Section 1(b) filing basis
6. Granting of application
7. Creating an ID to goods and services
8. Symbol identifying a brand (words/design)
12. United States Patent & Trademark Office

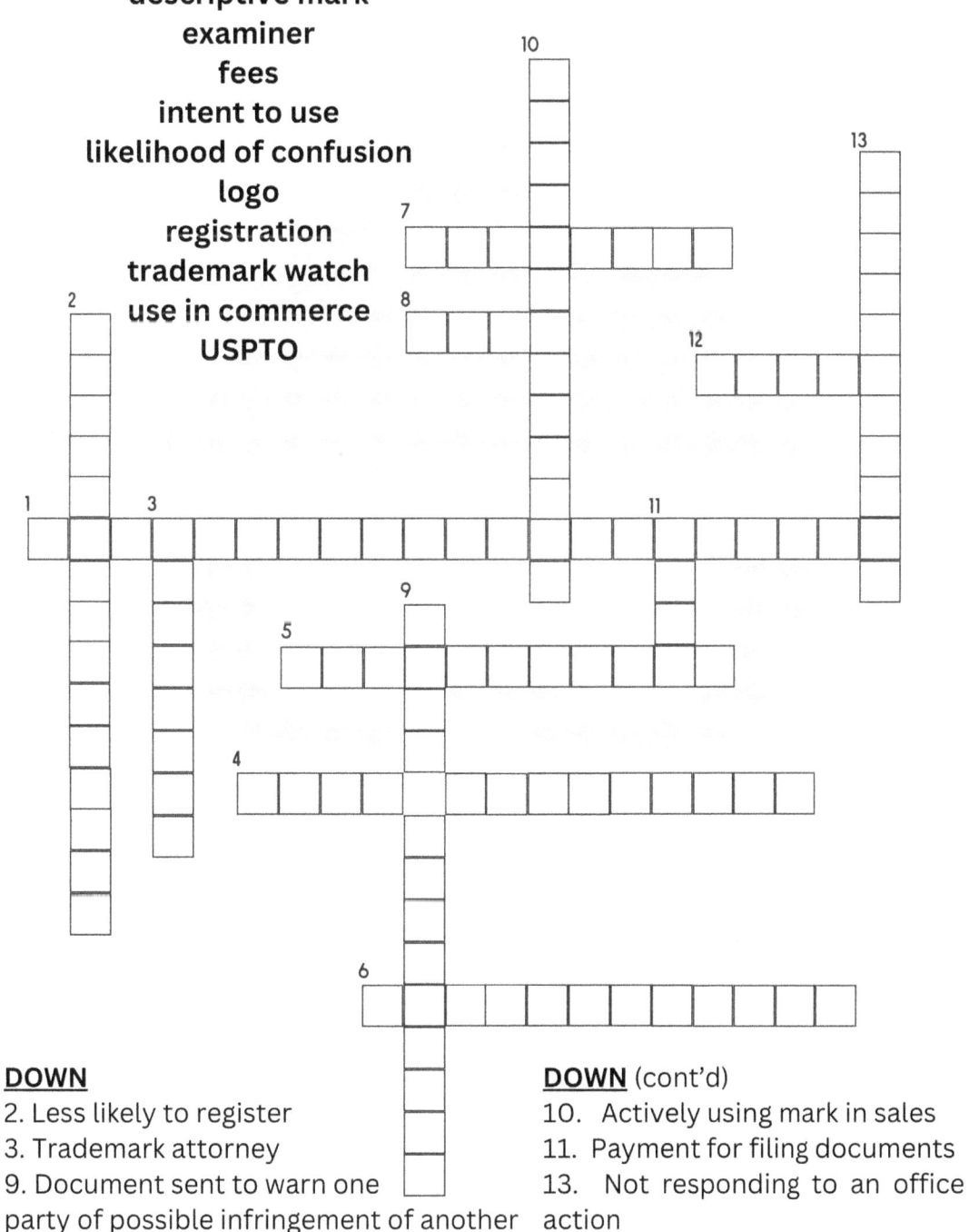

abandonment
branding
cease and desist
descriptive mark
examiner
fees
intent to use
likelihood of confusion
logo
registration
trademark watch
use in commerce
USPTO

DOWN
2. Less likely to register
3. Trademark attorney
9. Document sent to warn one party of possible infringement of another

DOWN (cont'd)
10. Actively using mark in sales
11. Payment for filing documents
13. Not responding to an office action

Intellectual Property DIY Trademarks | APPLICATION PROCESS

IP PUNCH LIST ™

THE APPLICATION – YOU CAN DIY

REMEMBER: Review TEAS Nuts & Bolts videos during application process

- ☐ Go to USPTO.gov
- ☐ LOGIN with your USER ID
- ☐ MENU=>Trademarks => Appl. Process =>Apply Online
- ☐ Initial application forms- (click to proceed)
- ☐ Note: There are 5 possible application forms. The first (main) application has two filing options, TEAS plus and TEAS standard. Option 2 thru 5 (see "other initial application forms") are for **SPECIFIC** use: certification, collective, collective membership. FYI
- ☐ If option 1...
  - TEAS plus OR standard
- ☐ Specimen (jpeg)
- ☐ • 1(a) OR 1(b)

BEFORE YOU SUBMIT

- ☐ * Validation page *
  - Input (review this)
  - Mark (shows drawing)
  - Specimen (shows file)
  - Text form (look it over)
- ☐ Pay/submit
- ☐ Record serial# on IP Planner
- ☐ If you get an OFFICE ACTION, don't panic. Follow instructions on how to reply OR call help desk.
- ☐ Record registration # once reg. is granted

APPLICATION PROCESS   Intellectual Property DIY Trademarks

Word Mark, slogan, etc.	Date filed	Class(es)	Amount paid	Serial #	Between year 5 & 6	Between year 9 & 10	10 years after last regis.
1.							
2.							
3.							
4.							

Registration #	Registration date	If Office Action	Amount spent	Further Office Action	Further amount spent	Other OA date	Other OA date	Other OA date	10 years after last regis. DEAD
1.									
2.									
3.									
4.									

IP PLANNER™

Intellectual Property DIY Trademarks — APPLICATION PROCESS

Word Mark, slogan, etc.	Date filed	Class(es)	Amount paid	Serial #	Between year 5 & 6	Between year 9 & 10	Between 10 years after last regis.	10 years after last regis.
1.								
2.								
3.								
4.								

	Registration #	Registration date	If Office Action	Amount spent	Further Office Action	Further amount spent	Other OA date	Other OA date	Other OA date	DEAD
1.										
2.										
3.										
4.										

IP PLANNER™

APPLICATION PROCESS Intellectual Property DIY Trademarks

IP PLANNER™

Word Mark, slogan, etc.	Date filed	Class(es)	Amount paid	Serial #	Between year 5 & 6	Between year 9 & 10	Between 10 years after last regis.	10 years after last regis.
1.								
2.								
3.								
4.								

Registration #	Registration date	If Office Action	Amount spent	Further Office Action	Further amount spent	Other OA date	Other OA date	Other OA date	DEAD
1.									
2.									
3.									
4.									

Intellectual Property DIY Trademarks — APPLICATION PROCESS

Word Mark, slogan, etc.	Date filed	Class(es)	Amount paid	Serial #	Between year 5 & 6	Between year 9 & 10	10 years after last regis.	10 years after last regis.
1.								
2.								
3.								
4.								

	Registration #	Registration date	If Office Action	Amount spent	Further Office Action	Further amount spent	Other OA date	Other OA date	Other OA date	DEAD
1.										
2.										
3.										
4.										

IP PLANNER™

APPLICATION PROCESS — Intellectual Property DIY Trademarks

Word Mark, slogan, etc.	Date filed	Class(es)	Amount paid	Serial #	Between year 5 & 6	Between year 9 & 10	Between 10 years after last regis.	10 years after last regis.
1.								
2.								
3.								
4.								

Registration #	Registration date	If Office Action	Amount spent	Further Office Action	Further amount spent	Other OA date	Other OA date	Other OA date	DEAD
1.									
2.									
3.									
4.									

IP PLANNER™

OFFICE ACTIONS

So, you got an office action? Don't throw in the towel. Even attorneys get office actions. The office action could be something as simple as the examining attorney needing a different screenshot that you submitted as a specimen. Whatever the case, the office action will be very specific on what the examining attorney has challenged. Take a deep breath and READ for a clear understanding of what they are asking from you. All is not lost. You will be allowed to respond and resubmit the information being requested. **DON'T GIVE UP**.

No office action is identical. It sometimes can be resolved rather quickly. Other times, you may need to seek legal help. Before hiring a lawyer, seek out help through the resources listed on USPTO.gov.

I'M A WITNESS. YOU GOT THIS.

MAINTENANCE

After all you went through to receive registration of your trademark, the last thing you want to do is lose it. I created the **IP PLANNER**™ *log sheet* so that you can see, at a glance, what trademarks you have applied for and when the fees are due for renewal. Stay connected to USPTO.gov for the most updated information concerning renewal dates and fees.

EXTRA SETS

IP PLANNER
&
PUNCH LIST ™

IP PUNCH LIST™

FIRST THINGS FIRST – THE RESOURCES

TRADEMARK ASSISTANCE CENTER

You're not alone in this. If you get stuck, reach out to the USPTO by phone or email. However, they WILL NOT give legal advice.

- ☐ USPTO.gov
  Menu ==> Trademarks => More Trademarks ==> Contact Trademarks
- ☐ Phone: 1-800-786-9199
- ☐ TrademarkAssistanceCenter@uspto.gov

TRADEMARK BASICS REGISTRATION TOOLKIT

START HERE! This document is FULL of information to assist you in the learning phase.

- ☐ What is a trademark
- ☐ Put public on notice
- ☐ Trademark symbols
- ☐ Trademark process
- ☐ Do I need an attorney?
- ☐ Conduct a search
- ☐ Application process
- ☐ Maintenance

and more...

Menu ==> Trademarks ==> Getting Started ==> Trademark Basics (scroll down)

TRADEMARK BASICS BOOT CAMP

More resources at USPTO.gov

LIVE presentations - 8 modules

- ☐ Fundamentals
- ☐ Registration process
- ☐ Searching
- ☐ Application
- ☐ Application filing
- ☐ Responding to office action
- ☐ Maintenance
- ☐ Q & A panel

and more...

Menu ==> Trademarks ==> Getting Started ==> Trademark Basics (scroll down)

VIDEOS - TEAS NUTS & BOLTS

Due to an update to the "search" system (11/23), some USPTO tutorial videos were removed and are being updated, at the time of printing this book. Review available videos BEFORE and DURING application process.

- ☐ TEAS Plus vs TEAS Standard
- ☐ Applicant Information
- ☐ Mark Drawing Page
- ☐ Additional Statements
- ☐ G & S TEAS Plus
- ☐ G & S TEAS Standard
- ☐ Filing Basis
- ☐ Correspondence Informaton
- ☐ Signature Information
- ☐ Validation Page

MENU ==> Trademarks ==> Application process ==> Apply online ==>Scroll down to Nuts & Bolts videos

and more...

TRADEMARK WORD SEARCH

Find and circle trademark related words

L	R	U	S	T	I	M	M	S	E	R	V	I	C	E	M	A	R	K	C
E	M	M	U	N	I	C	A	T	I	C	N	O	X	Y	H	G	E	7	U
G	T	I	L	I	B	9	T	A	P	L	O	C	R	E	Y	T	I	T	I
A	R	E	F	I	L	I	N	G	B	A	S	I	S	R	J	F	O	E	T
L	O	R	P	M	O	C	I	M	A	S	N	I	E	L	J	I	E	A	A
E	F	3	T	S	E	N	O	H	R	S	7	D	R	H	N	O	M	S	Y
N	A	C	U	S	T	S	U	E	P	O	R	T	V	P	E	F	R	P	S
T	X	P	I	Y	E	P	M	M	R	E	V	O	I	M	A	F	T	L	E
I	A	T	R	A	D	E	M	A	R	K	K	F	C	E	N	I	O	U	1
T	V	A	R	T	N	C	R	R	E	K	O	T	E	A	T	C	M	S	A
Y	I	T	A	C	T	I	T	I	M	M	R	T	S	A	R	E	T	I	M
P	E	C	R	E	P	M	E	R	D	N	Y	2	R	F	S	A	O	R	S
A	R	R	O	M	M	E	T	N	M	M	L	O	C	N	I	C	A	M	E
T	E	I	T	N	E	N	M	I	A	M	E	C	I	I	M	T	T	N	A
D	I	S	C	L	A	I	M	E	R	P	E	R	P	O	C	I	M	U	R
B	M	S	C	S	S	E	N	O	K	Y	T	I	L	A	P	O	R	T	C
I	S	S	C	A	R	T	S	E	M	O	G	O	O	D	S	N	O	D	H

CLASS	DISCLAIMER	FILING BASIS
GOODS	LEGAL ENTITY	MARK
OFFICE ACTION	SEARCH	SERVICE MARK
SERVICES	SPECIMEN	TAC
TEAS PLUS	TRADEMARK	1A

NOTES

Video title

IP PUNCH LIST™

SKETCH A LOGO OR DESIGN

IP PUNCH LIST ™

PREP WORK – THE SEARCH

- ☐ *Watch USPTO tutorials

- ☐ Do a BRAINSTORM exercise (see worksheet) to come up with 1-5 ideas for a mark, in case your idea is already registered.

Videos/FAQ's on searching
Menu ==>
Trademarks ==>
Application Proc. =>
Search Our Trademark Database

- ☐ An attorney would do an extensive SEARCH. The USPTO gives YOU guidance on how to search BEFORE you apply for your mark.

- ☐ SEARCH for mark being used in commerce (as per USPTO). Use included note paper.
  - search USPTO site
  - search on social media
  - search on Google
  - search on internet

- ☐ Do a BRAINSTORM exercise (see worksheet) to determine the International Class(es) in which you want to file your mark. ==> There is a FEE per CLASS. Must select at least 1 class

- ☐ Filing basis?
  - 1(a)
  - 1(b)
  - Other (per USPTO)

- ☐ Prep your specimen

*In November 2023, the USPTO updated to a new SEARCH system. At the time of printing this book, the "TEAS Nuts and Bolts" videos were available.

Brainstorm Exercise

You may already know what word(s) you want to file for a trademark. What if the word(s), slogan, etc. is already registered? Brainstorm 1-5 new options, as you prepare to SEARCH, according to USPTO recommendations.

WORD MARK, PHRASE, ETC.

☐

WORD MARK, PHRASE, ETC.

☐

WORD MARK, PHRASE, ETC.

☐

WORD MARK, PHRASE, ETC.

☐

WORD MARK, PHRASE, ETC.

☐

SEARCH NOTES

Brainstorm Exercise

Use this worksheet to plan which International Class(es) you want to file your mark under. **There is a FEE** for each class. You must choose at least 1 of the 45 classes. Refer to the TEAS Nuts & Bolts Goods & Services video that explains the ID manual. Remember: IN USE or INTENDED USE

☐ List goods/services IN USE or INTENDED USE
ex. socks, hoodies, combs, brushes

☐ List CLASS for each good/service
ex. 25, 21

☐ Notes

Word Mark	**IP PLANNER™ CARD**	
		Filing basis
	List goods/services	
Date First Use Anywhere: Date First Use In Commerce:		Class(es)

Word Mark	**IP PLANNER™ CARD**	
		Filing basis
	List goods/services	
Date First Use Anywhere: Date First Use In Commerce:		Class(es)

TRADEMARK CROSSWORD PUZZLE

abandonment
branding
cease and desist
descriptive mark
examiner
fees
intent to use
likelihood of confusion
logo
registration
trademark watch
use in commerce
USPTO

ACROSS
1. Similarity could cause rejection
4. Idea of self monitoring activity
5. Section 1(b) filing basis
6. Granting of application
7. Creating an ID to goods and services
8. Symbol identifying a brand (words/design)
12. United States Patent & Trademark Office

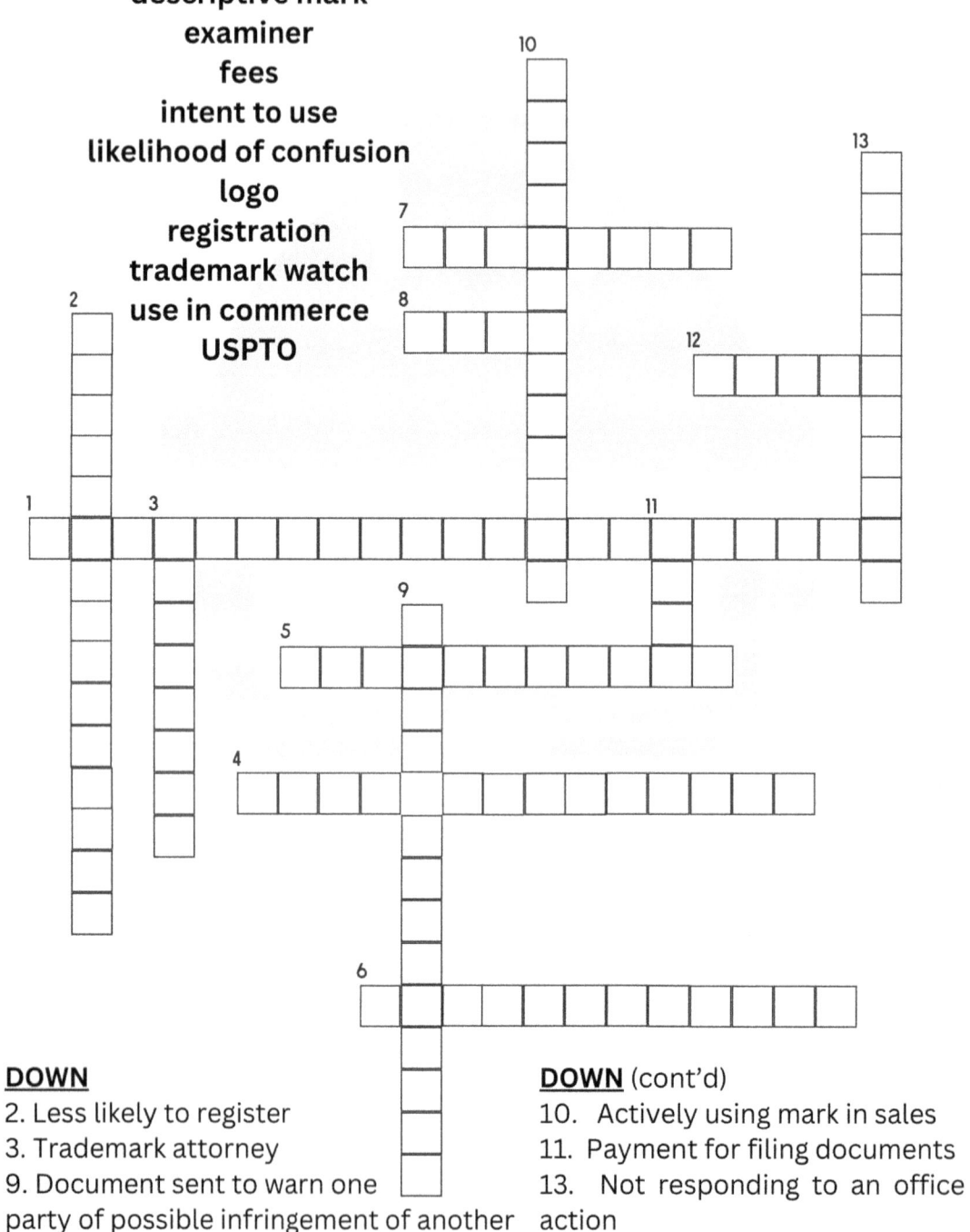

DOWN
2. Less likely to register
3. Trademark attorney
9. Document sent to warn one party of possible infringement of another

DOWN (cont'd)
10. Actively using mark in sales
11. Payment for filing documents
13. Not responding to an office action

IP PUNCH LIST ™

THE APPLICATION — YOU CAN DIY

REMEMBER: Review TEAS Nuts & Bolts videos during application process

- ☐ Go to USPTO.gov
- ☐ LOGIN with your USER ID
- ☐ MENU=>Trademarks => Appl. Process =>Apply Online
- ☐ Initial application forms- (click to proceed)
- ☐ Note: There are 5 possible application forms. The first (main) application has two filing options, TEAS plus and TEAS standard. Option 2 thru 5 (see "other initial application forms") are for **SPECIFIC** use: certification, collective, collective membership. FYI
- ☐ If option 1...
  - TEAS plus OR standard
- ☐ Specimen (jpeg)
- ☐ 1(a) OR 1(b)

BEFORE YOU SUBMIT

- ☐ * Validation page *
  - Input (review this)
  - Mark (shows drawing)
  - Specimen (shows file)
  - Text form (look it over)
- ☐ Pay/submit
- ☐ Record serial# on IP Planner
- ☐ If you get an OFFICE ACTION, don't panic. Follow instructions on how to reply OR call help desk.
- ☐ Record registration # once reg. is granted

IP PUNCH LIST™

FIRST THINGS FIRST – THE RESOURCES

TRADEMARK ASSISTANCE CENTER

You're not alone in this. If you get stuck, reach out to the USPTO by phone or email. However, they WILL NOT give legal advice.

- ☐ USPTO.gov
  Menu ==> Trademarks => More Trademarks ==> Contact Trademarks
- ☐ Phone: 1-800-786-9199
- ☐ TrademarkAssistanceCenter@uspto.gov

TRADEMARK BASICS REGISTRATION TOOLKIT

START HERE! This document is FULL of information to assist you in the learning phase.

- ☐ What is a trademark
- ☐ Put public on notice
- ☐ Trademark symbols
- ☐ Trademark process
- ☐ Do I need an attorney?
- ☐ Conduct a search
- ☐ Application process
- ☐ Maintenance *and more...*

Menu ==> Trademarks ==> Getting Started ==> Trademark Basics (scroll down)

TRADEMARK BASICS BOOT CAMP

More resources at USPTO.gov

LIVE presentations - 8 modules

- ☐ Fundamentals
- ☐ Registration process
- ☐ Searching
- ☐ Application
- ☐ Application filing
- ☐ Responding to office action
- ☐ Maintenance
- ☐ Q & A panel *and more...*

Menu ==> Trademarks ==> Getting Started ==> Trademark Basics (scroll down)

VIDEOS - TEAS NUTS & BOLTS

Due to an update to the "search" system (11/23), some USPTO tutorial videos were removed and are being updated, at the time of printing this book. Review available videos BEFORE and DURING application process.

- ☐ TEAS Plus vs TEAS Standard
- ☐ Applicant Information
- ☐ Mark Drawing Page
- ☐ Additional Statements
- ☐ G & S TEAS Plus
- ☐ G & S TEAS Standard
- ☐ Filing Basis
- ☐ Correspondence Informaton
- ☐ Signature Information
- ☐ Validation Page

MENU ==> Trademarks ==> Application process ==> Apply online ==>Scroll down to Nuts & Bolts videos

and more...

TRADEMARK WORD SEARCH

Find and circle trademark related words

L	R	U	S	T	I	M	M	S	E	R	V	I	C	E	M	A	R	K	C
E	M	M	U	N	I	C	A	T	I	C	N	O	X	Y	H	G	E	7	U
G	T	I	L	I	B	9	T	A	P	L	O	C	R	E	Y	T	I	T	I
A	R	E	F	I	L	I	N	G	B	A	S	I	S	R	J	F	O	E	T
L	O	R	P	M	O	C	I	M	A	S	N	I	E	L	J	I	E	A	A
E	F	3	T	S	E	N	O	H	R	S	7	D	R	H	N	O	M	S	Y
N	A	C	U	S	T	S	U	E	P	O	R	T	V	P	E	F	R	P	S
T	X	P	I	Y	E	P	M	M	R	E	V	O	I	M	A	F	T	L	E
I	A	T	R	A	D	E	M	A	R	K	K	F	C	E	N	I	O	U	1
T	V	A	R	T	N	C	R	R	E	K	O	T	E	A	T	C	M	S	A
Y	I	T	A	C	T	I	T	I	M	M	R	T	S	A	R	E	T	I	M
P	E	C	R	E	P	M	E	R	D	N	Y	2	R	F	S	A	O	R	S
A	R	R	O	M	M	E	T	N	M	M	L	O	C	N	I	C	A	M	E
T	C	I	T	N	C	N	M	I	A	M	E	C	I	I	M	T	T	N	A
D	I	S	C	L	A	I	M	E	R	P	E	R	P	O	C	I	M	U	R
B	M	S	C	S	S	E	N	O	K	Y	T	I	L	A	P	O	R	T	C
I	S	S	C	A	R	T	S	E	M	O	G	O	O	D	S	N	O	D	H

CLASS	DISCLAIMER	FILING BASIS
GOODS	LEGAL ENTITY	MARK
OFFICE ACTION	SEARCH	SERVICE MARK
SERVICES	SPECIMEN	TAC
TEAS PLUS	TRADEMARK	1A

NOTES

Video title _____

IP PUNCH LIST™

SKETCH A LOGO OR DESIGN

IP PUNCH LIST ™

PREP WORK – THE SEARCH

- ☐ *Watch USPTO tutorials

- ☐ Do a BRAINSTORM exercise (see worksheet) to come up with 1-5 ideas for a mark, in case your idea is already registered.

- ☐ An attorney would do an extensive SEARCH. The USPTO gives YOU guidance on how to search BEFORE you apply for your mark.

Videos/FAQ's on searching
Menu ==>
Trademarks ==>
Application Proc. =>
Search Our Trademark Database

- ☐ SEARCH for mark being used in commerce (as per USPTO). Use included note paper.
  - search USPTO site
  - search on social media
  - search on Google
  - search on internet

- ☐ Do a BRAINSTORM exercise (see worksheet) to determine the International Class(es) in which you want to file your mark. ==> There is a FEE per CLASS. Must select at least 1 class

- ☐ Filing basis?
  - 1(a)
  - 1(b)
  - Other (per USPTO)

- ☐ Prep your specimen

*In November 2023, the USPTO updated to a new SEARCH system. At the time of printing this book, the "TEAS Nuts and Bolts" videos were available.

Brainstorm Exercise

You may already know what word(s) you want to file for a trademark. What if the word(s), slogan, etc. is already registered? Brainstorm 1-5 new options, as you prepare to SEARCH, according to USPTO recommendations.

WORD MARK, PHRASE, ETC.

☐

WORD MARK, PHRASE, ETC.

☐

WORD MARK, PHRASE, ETC.

☐

WORD MARK, PHRASE, ETC.

☐

WORD MARK, PHRASE, ETC.

☐

SEARCH NOTES

Brainstorm Exercise

Use this worksheet to plan which International Class(es) you want to file your mark under. **There is a FEE** for each class. You must choose at least 1 of the 45 classes. Refer to the TEAS Nuts & Bolts Goods & Services video that explains the ID manual. Remember: IN USE or INTENDED USE

List goods/services IN USE or INTENDED USE
ex. socks, hoodies, combs, brushes

☐

List CLASS for each good/service
ex. 25, 21

☐

Notes

☐

Word Mark	IP PLANNER™ CARD	
		Filing basis
List goods/services		
Date First Use Anywhere: Date First Use In Commerce:		Class(es)

Word Mark	IP PLANNER™ CARD	
		Filing basis
List goods/services		
Date First Use Anywhere: Date First Use In Commerce:		Class(es)

TRADEMARK CROSSWORD PUZZLE

ACROSS
1. Similarity could cause rejection
4. Idea of self monitoring activity
5. Section 1(b) filing basis
6. Granting of application
7. Creating an ID to goods and services
8. Symbol identifying a brand (words/design)
12. United States Patent & Trademark Office

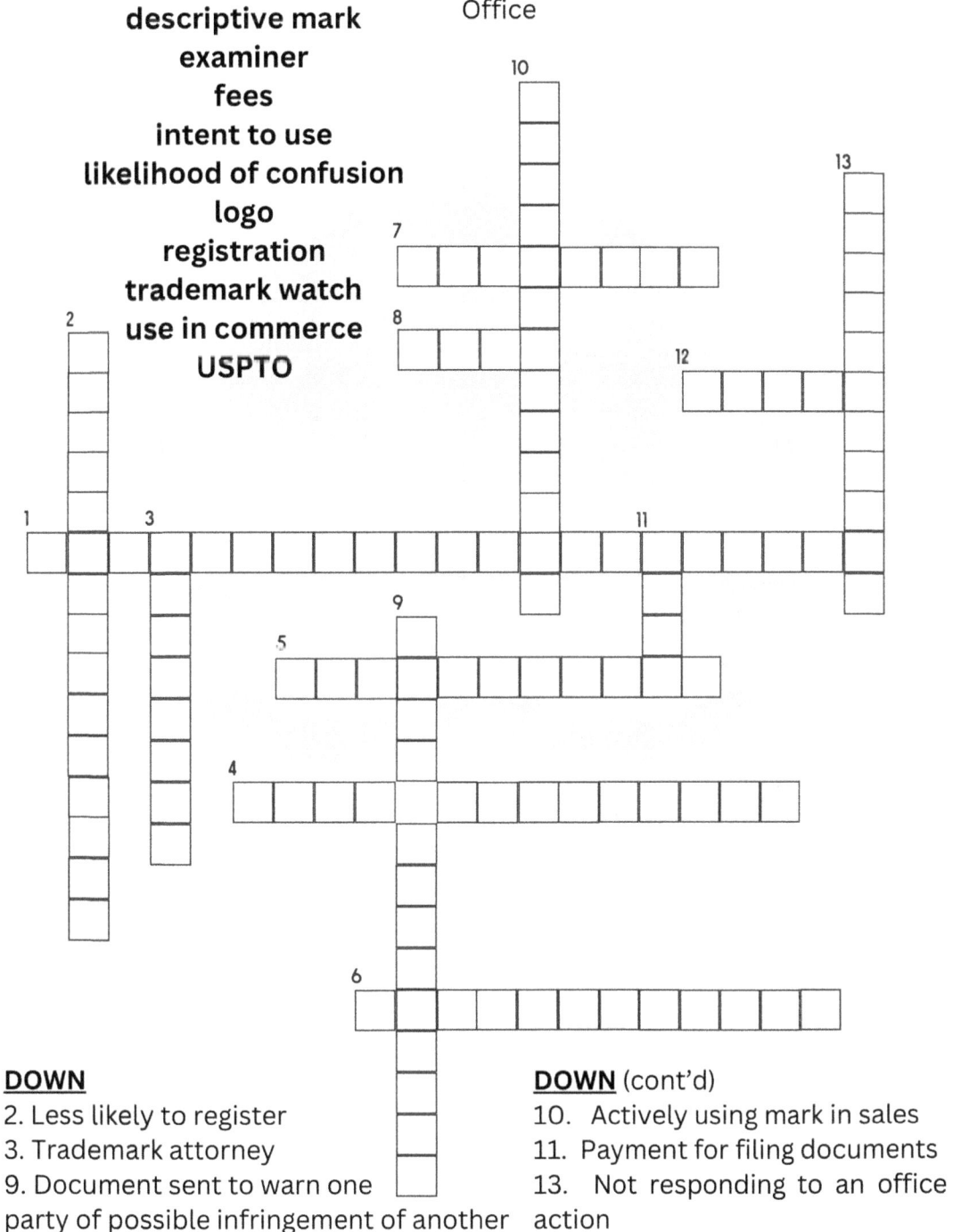

abandonment
branding
cease and desist
descriptive mark
examiner
fees
intent to use
likelihood of confusion
logo
registration
trademark watch
use in commerce
USPTO

DOWN
2. Less likely to register
3. Trademark attorney
9. Document sent to warn one party of possible infringement of another

DOWN (cont'd)
10. Actively using mark in sales
11. Payment for filing documents
13. Not responding to an office action

IP PUNCH LIST ™

THE APPLICATION – YOU CAN DIY

REMEMBER: Review TEAS Nuts & Bolts videos during application process

- ☐ Go to USPTO.gov
- ☐ LOGIN with your USER ID
- ☐ MENU=>Trademarks => Appl. Process =>Apply Online
- ☐ Initial application forms- (click to proceed)
- ☐ Note: There are 5 possible application forms. The first (main) application has two filing options, TEAS plus and TEAS standard. Option 2 thru 5 (see "other initial application forms") are for **SPECIFIC** use: certification, collective, collective membership. FYI
- ☐ If option 1...
  - TEAS plus OR standard
- ☐ Specimen (jpeg)
- ☐ • 1(a) OR 1(b)

BEFORE YOU SUBMIT

- ☐ * Validation page *
- ☐ • Input (review this)
  - Mark (shows drawing)
  - Specimen (shows file)
  - Text form (look it over)
- ☐ Pay/submit
- ☐ Record serial# on IP Planner
- ☐ If you get an OFFICE ACTION, don't panic. Follow instructions on how to reply OR call help desk.
- ☐ Record registration # once reg. is granted

IP PUNCH LIST™

FIRST THINGS FIRST – THE RESOURCES

TRADEMARK ASSISTANCE CENTER

You're not alone in this. If you get stuck, reach out to the USPTO by phone or email. However, they WILL NOT give legal advice.

- ☐ USPTO.gov
  Menu ==> Trademarks => More Trademarks ==> Contact Trademarks
- ☐ Phone: 1-800-786-9199
- ☐ TrademarkAssistanceCenter@uspto.gov

TRADEMARK BASICS REGISTRATION TOOLKIT

START HERE! This document is FULL of information to assist you in the learning phase.

- ☐ What is a trademark
- ☐ Put public on notice
- ☐ Trademark symbols
- ☐ Trademark process
- ☐ Do I need an attorney?
- ☐ Conduct a search
- ☐ Application process
- ☐ Maintenance

and more...

Menu ==> Trademarks ==> Getting Started ==> Trademark Basics (scroll down)

TRADEMARK BASICS BOOT CAMP

More resources at USPTO.gov

LIVE presentations - 8 modules

- ☐ Fundamentals
- ☐ Registration process
- ☐ Searching
- ☐ Application
- ☐ Application filing
- ☐ Responding to office action
- ☐ Maintenance
- ☐ Q & A panel

and more...

Menu ==> Trademarks ==> Getting Started ==> Trademark Basics (scroll down)

VIDEOS - TEAS NUTS & BOLTS

Due to an update to the "search" system (11/23), some USPTO tutorial videos were removed and are being updated, at the time of printing this book. Review available videos BEFORE and DURING application process.

- ☐ TEAS Plus vs TEAS Standard
- ☐ Applicant Information
- ☐ Mark Drawing Page
- ☐ Additional Statements
- ☐ G & S TEAS Plus
- ☐ G & S TEAS Standard
- ☐ Filing Basis
- ☐ Correspondence Informaton
- ☐ Signature Information
- ☐ Validation Page

MENU ==> Trademarks ==> Application process ==> Apply online ==>Scroll down to Nuts & Bolts videos

and more...

TRADEMARK WORD SEARCH

Find and circle trademark related words

L	R	U	S	T	I	M	M	S	E	R	V	I	C	E	M	A	R	K	C
E	M	M	U	N	I	C	A	T	I	C	N	O	X	Y	H	G	E	7	U
G	T	I	L	I	B	9	T	A	P	L	O	C	R	E	Y	T	I	T	I
A	R	E	F	I	L	I	N	G	B	A	S	I	S	R	J	F	O	E	T
L	O	R	P	M	O	C	I	M	A	S	N	I	E	L	J	I	E	A	A
E	F	3	T	S	E	N	O	H	R	S	7	D	R	H	N	O	M	S	Y
N	A	C	U	S	T	S	U	E	P	O	R	T	V	P	E	F	R	P	S
T	X	P	I	Y	E	P	M	M	R	E	V	O	I	M	A	F	T	L	E
I	A	T	R	A	D	E	M	A	R	K	K	F	C	E	N	I	O	U	1
T	V	A	R	T	N	C	R	R	E	K	O	T	E	A	T	C	M	S	A
Y	I	T	A	C	T	I	T	I	M	M	R	T	S	A	R	E	T	I	M
P	E	C	R	E	P	M	E	R	D	N	Y	2	R	F	S	A	O	R	S
A	R	R	O	M	M	E	T	N	M	M	L	O	C	N	I	C	A	M	E
T	E	I	T	N	E	N	M	I	A	M	E	C	I	I	M	T	T	N	A
D	I	S	C	L	A	I	M	E	R	P	E	R	P	O	C	I	M	U	R
B	M	S	C	S	S	E	N	O	K	Y	T	I	L	A	P	O	R	T	C
I	S	S	C	A	R	T	S	E	M	O	G	O	O	D	S	N	O	D	H

CLASS	DISCLAIMER	FILING BASIS
GOODS	LEGAL ENTITY	MARK
OFFICE ACTION	SEARCH	SERVICE MARK
SERVICES	SPECIMEN	TAC
TEAS PLUS	TRADEMARK	1A

NOTES

Video title

IP PUNCH LIST™

SKETCH A LOGO OR DESIGN

IP PUNCH LIST™

PREP WORK – THE SEARCH

- ☐ *Watch USPTO tutorials

- ☐ Do a BRAINSTORM exercise (see worksheet) to come up with 1-5 ideas for a mark, in case your idea is already registered.

- ☐ An attorney would do an extensive SEARCH. The USPTO gives YOU guidance on how to search BEFORE you apply for your mark.

Videos/FAQ's on searching
Menu ==>
Trademarks ==>
Application Proc. =>
Search Our Trademark Database

- ☐ SEARCH for mark being used in commerce (as per USPTO). Use included note paper.
  - search USPTO site
  - search on social media
  - search on Google
  - search on internet

- ☐ Do a BRAINSTORM exercise (see worksheet) to determine the International Class(es) in which you want to file your mark. ==> There is a FEE per CLASS. Must select at least 1 class

- ☐ Filing basis?
  - 1(a)
  - 1(b)
  - Other (per USPTO)

- ☐ Prep your specimen

*In November 2023, the USPTO updated to a new SEARCH system. At the time of printing this book, the "TEAS Nuts and Bolts" videos were available.

Brainstorm Exercise

You may already know what word(s) you want to file for a trademark. What if the word(s), slogan, etc. is already registered? Brainstorm 1-5 new options, as you prepare to SEARCH, according to USPTO recommendations.

WORD MARK, PHRASE, ETC.

☐

WORD MARK, PHRASE, ETC.

☐

WORD MARK, PHRASE, ETC.

☐

WORD MARK, PHRASE, ETC.

☐

WORD MARK, PHRASE, ETC.

☐

SEARCH NOTES

Brainstorm Exercise

Use this worksheet to plan which International Class(es) you want to file your mark under. **There is a FEE** for each class. You must choose at least 1 of the 45 classes. Refer to the TEAS Nuts & Bolts Goods & Services video that explains the ID manual. Remember: IN USE or INTENDED USE

☐ List goods/services IN USE or INTENDED USE
ex. socks, hoodies, combs, brushes

☐ List CLASS for each good/service
ex. 25, 21

☐ Notes

Word Mark	IP PLANNER™ CARD	
		Filing basis
List goods/services		
Date First Use Anywhere: Date First Use In Commerce:		Class(es)

Word Mark	IP PLANNER™ CARD	
		Filing basis
List goods/services		
Date First Use Anywhere: Date First Use In Commerce:		Class(es)

TRADEMARK CROSSWORD PUZZLE

abandonment
branding
cease and desist
descriptive mark
examiner
fees
intent to use
likelihood of confusion
logo
registration
trademark watch
use in commerce
USPTO

ACROSS
1. Similarity could cause rejection
4. Idea of self monitoring activity
5. Section 1(b) filing basis
6. Granting of application
7. Creating an ID to goods and services
8. Symbol identifying a brand (words/design)
12. United States Patent & Trademark Office

DOWN
2. Less likely to register
3. Trademark attorney
9. Document sent to warn one party of possible infringement of another

DOWN (cont'd)
10. Actively using mark in sales
11. Payment for filing documents
13. Not responding to an office action

IP PUNCH LIST ™

THE APPLICATION – YOU CAN DIY

REMEMBER: Review TEAS Nuts & Bolts videos during application process

- ☐ Go to USPTO.gov
- ☐ LOGIN with your USER ID
- ☐ MENU=>Trademarks => Appl. Process =>Apply Online
- ☐ Initial application forms- (click to proceed)
- ☐ Note: There are 5 possible application forms. The first (main) application has two filing options, TEAS plus and TEAS standard. Option 2 thru 5 (see "other initial application forms") are for **SPECIFIC** use: certification, collective, collective membership. FYI
- ☐ If option 1...
  - TEAS plus OR standard
- ☐ Specimen (jpeg)
- ☐ 1(a) OR 1(b)

BEFORE YOU SUBMIT

- ☐ * Validation page *
- • Input (review this)
- • Mark (shows drawing)
- • Specimen (shows file)
- • Text form (look it over)
- ☐ Pay/submit
- ☐ Record serial# on IP Planner
- ☐ If you get an OFFICE ACTION, don't panic. Follow instructions on how to reply OR call help desk.
- ☐ Record registration # once reg. is granted

IP PUNCH LIST ™

FIRST THINGS FIRST – THE RESOURCES

TRADEMARK ASSISTANCE CENTER

You're not alone in this. If you get stuck, reach out to the USPTO by phone or email. However, they WILL NOT give legal advice.

- ☐ USPTO.gov
  Menu ==> Trademarks => More Trademarks ==> Contact Trademarks
- ☐ Phone: 1-800-786-9199
- ☐ TrademarkAssistanceCenter@uspto.gov

TRADEMARK BASICS REGISTRATION TOOLKIT

START HERE! This document is FULL of information to assist you in the learning phase.

- ☐ What is a trademark
- ☐ Put public on notice
- ☐ Trademark symbols
- ☐ Trademark process
- ☐ Do I need an attorney?
- ☐ Conduct a search
- ☐ Application process
- ☐ Maintenance

and more...

Menu ==> Trademarks ==> Getting Started ==> Trademark Basics (scroll down)

TRADEMARK BASICS BOOT CAMP

More resources at USPTO.gov

LIVE presentations - 8 modules

- ☐ Fundamentals
- ☐ Registration process
- ☐ Searching
- ☐ Application
- ☐ Application filing
- ☐ Responding to office action
- ☐ Maintenance
- ☐ Q & A panel

and more...

Menu ==> Trademarks ==> Getting Started ==> Trademark Basics (scroll down)

VIDEOS - TEAS NUTS & BOLTS

Due to an update to the "search" system (11/23), some USPTO tutorial videos were removed and are being updated, at the time of printing this book. Review available videos BEFORE and DURING application process.

- ☐ TEAS Plus vs TEAS Standard
- ☐ Applicant Information
- ☐ Mark Drawing Page
- ☐ Additional Statements
- ☐ G & S TEAS Plus
- ☐ G & S TEAS Standard
- ☐ Filing Basis
- ☐ Correspondence Informaton
- ☐ Signature Information
- ☐ Validation Page

MENU ==> Trademarks ==> Application process ==> Apply online ==>Scroll down to Nuts & Bolts videos

and more...

TRADEMARK WORD SEARCH

Find and circle trademark related words

L	R	U	S	T	I	M	M	S	E	R	V	I	C	E	M	A	R	K	C
E	M	M	U	N	I	C	A	T	I	C	N	O	X	Y	H	G	E	7	U
G	T	I	L	I	B	9	T	A	P	L	O	C	R	E	Y	T	I	T	I
A	R	E	F	I	L	I	N	G	B	A	S	I	S	R	J	F	O	E	T
L	O	R	P	M	O	C	I	M	A	S	N	I	E	L	J	I	E	A	A
E	F	3	T	S	E	N	O	H	R	S	7	D	R	H	N	O	M	S	Y
N	A	C	U	S	T	S	U	E	P	O	R	T	V	P	E	F	R	P	S
T	X	P	I	Y	E	P	M	M	R	E	V	O	I	M	A	F	T	L	E
I	A	T	R	A	D	E	M	A	R	K	K	F	C	E	N	I	O	U	1
T	V	A	R	T	N	C	R	R	E	K	O	T	E	A	T	C	M	S	A
Y	I	T	A	C	T	I	T	I	M	M	R	T	S	A	R	E	T	I	M
P	E	C	R	E	P	M	E	R	D	N	Y	2	R	F	S	A	O	R	S
A	R	R	O	M	M	E	T	N	M	M	L	O	C	N	I	C	A	M	E
T	E	I	T	N	E	N	M	I	A	M	E	C	I	I	M	T	T	N	A
D	I	S	C	L	A	I	M	E	R	P	E	R	P	O	C	I	M	U	R
B	M	S	C	S	S	E	N	O	K	Y	T	I	L	A	P	O	R	T	C
I	S	S	C	A	R	T	S	E	M	O	G	O	O	D	S	N	O	D	H

CLASS	DISCLAIMER	FILING BASIS
GOODS	LEGAL ENTITY	MARK
OFFICE ACTION	SEARCH	SERVICE MARK
SERVICES	SPECIMEN	TAC
TEAS PLUS	TRADEMARK	1A

NOTES

Video title _____

IP PUNCH LIST™

SKETCH A LOGO OR DESIGN

IP PUNCH LIST ™

PREP WORK – THE SEARCH

- ☐ *Watch USPTO tutorials

- ☐ Do a BRAINSTORM exercise (see worksheet) to come up with 1-5 ideas for a mark, in case your idea is already registered.

- ☐ An attorney would do an extensive SEARCH. The USPTO gives YOU guidance on how to search BEFORE you apply for your mark.

Videos/FAQ's on searching
Menu ==>
Trademarks ==>
Application Proc. =>
Search Our Trademark Database

- ☐ SEARCH for mark being used in commerce (as per USPTO). Use included note paper.
  - search USPTO site
  - search on social media
  - search on Google
  - search on internet

- ☐ Do a BRAINSTORM exercise (see worksheet) to determine the International Class(es) in which you want to file your mark. ==> There is a FEE per CLASS. Must select at least 1 class

- ☐ Filing basis?
  - 1(a)
  - 1(b)
  - Other (per USPTO)

- ☐ Prep your specimen

*In November 2023, the USPTO updated to a new SEARCH system. At the time of printing this book, the "TEAS Nuts and Bolts" videos were available.

Brainstorm Exercise

You may already know what word(s) you want to file for a trademark. What if the word(s), slogan, etc. is already registered? Brainstorm 1-5 new options, as you prepare to SEARCH, according to USPTO recommendations.

WORD MARK, PHRASE, ETC.

☐

WORD MARK, PHRASE, ETC.

☐

WORD MARK, PHRASE, ETC.

☐

WORD MARK, PHRASE, ETC.

☐

WORD MARK, PHRASE, ETC.

☐

SEARCH NOTES

Brainstorm Exercise

Use this worksheet to plan which International Class(es) you want to file your mark under. **There is a FEE** for each class. You must choose at least 1 of the 45 classes. Refer to the TEAS Nuts & Bolts Goods & Services video that explains the ID manual. Remember: IN USE or INTENDED USE

List goods/services IN USE or INTENDED USE
ex. socks, hoodies, combs, brushes

☐

List CLASS for each good/service
ex. 25, 21

☐

Notes

☐

Word Mark	IP PLANNER™ CARD	
		Filing basis
List goods/services		
Date First Use Anywhere: Date First Use In Commerce:		Class(es)

Word Mark	IP PLANNER™ CARD	
		Filing basis
List goods/services		
Date First Use Anywhere: Date First Use In Commerce:		Class(es)

TRADEMARK CROSSWORD PUZZLE

Word Bank:
- abandonment
- branding
- cease and desist
- descriptive mark
- examiner
- fees
- intent to use
- likelihood of confusion
- logo
- registration
- trademark watch
- use in commerce
- USPTO

ACROSS
1. Similarity could cause rejection
4. Idea of self monitoring activity
5. Section 1(b) filing basis
6. Granting of application
7. Creating an ID to goods and services
8. Symbol identifying a brand (words/design)
12. United States Patent & Trademark Office

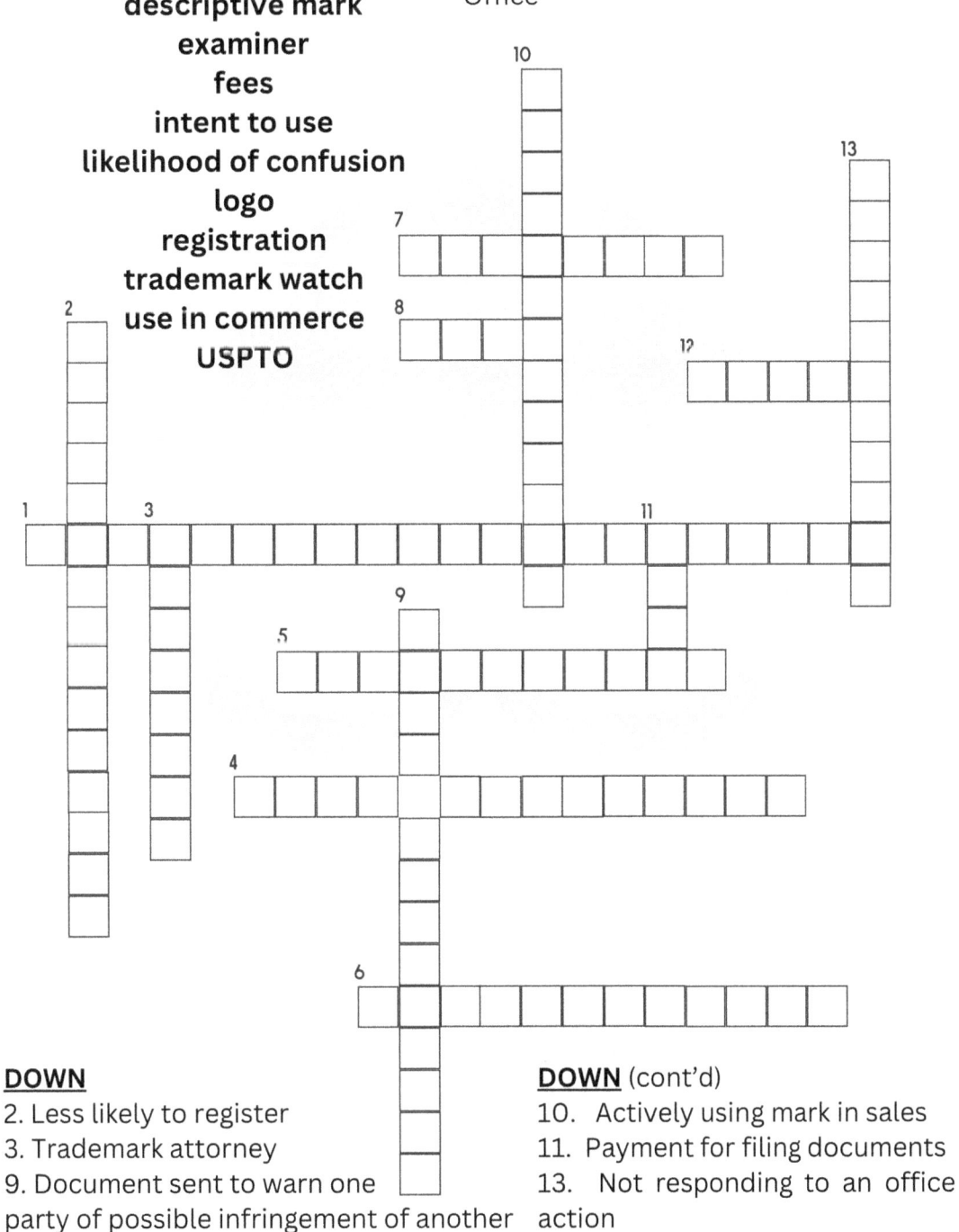

DOWN
2. Less likely to register
3. Trademark attorney
9. Document sent to warn one party of possible infringement of another

DOWN (cont'd)
10. Actively using mark in sales
11. Payment for filing documents
13. Not responding to an office action

IP PUNCH LIST ™

THE APPLICATION – YOU CAN DIY

REMEMBER: Review TEAS Nuts & Bolts videos during application process

- ☐ Go to USPTO.gov
- ☐ LOGIN with your USER ID
- ☐ MENU=>Trademarks => Appl. Process =>Apply Online
- ☐ Initial application forms- (click to proceed)
- ☐ Note: There are 5 possible application forms. The first (main) application has two filing options, TEAS plus and TEAS standard. Option 2 thru 5 (see "other initial application forms") are for **SPECIFIC** use: certification, collective, collective membership. FYI
- ☐ If option 1...
  - TEAS plus OR standard
- ☐ Specimen (jpeg)
- ☐ • 1(a) OR 1(b)

BEFORE YOU SUBMIT

- ☐ * Validation page *
- • Input (review this)
- • Mark (shows drawing)
- • Specimen (shows file)
- • Text form (look it over)
- ☐ Pay/submit
- ☐ Record serial# on IP Planner
- ☐ If you get an OFFICE ACTION, don't panic. Follow instructions on how to reply OR call help desk.
- ☐ Record registration # once reg. is granted

IP PUNCH LIST™

FIRST THINGS FIRST – THE RESOURCES

TRADEMARK ASSISTANCE CENTER

You're not alone in this. If you get stuck, reach out to the USPTO by phone or email. However, they WILL NOT give legal advice.

- ☐ USPTO.gov
  Menu ==> Trademarks => More Trademarks ==> Contact Trademarks
- ☐ Phone: 1-800-786-9199
- ☐ TrademarkAssistanceCenter@uspto.gov

TRADEMARK BASICS REGISTRATION TOOLKIT

START HERE! This document is FULL of information to assist you in the learning phase.

- ☐ What is a trademark
- ☐ Put public on notice
- ☐ Trademark symbols
- ☐ Trademark process
- ☐ Do I need an attorney?
- ☐ Conduct a search
- ☐ Application process
- ☐ Maintenance

and more...

Menu ==> Trademarks ==> Getting Started ==> Trademark Basics (scroll down)

TRADEMARK BASICS BOOT CAMP

More resources at USPTO.gov

LIVE presentations - 8 modules

- ☐ Fundamentals
- ☐ Registration process
- ☐ Searching
- ☐ Application
- ☐ Application filing
- ☐ Responding to office action
- ☐ Maintenance
- ☐ Q & A panel

and more...

Menu ==> Trademarks ==> Getting Started ==> Trademark Basics (scroll down)

VIDEOS - TEAS NUTS & BOLTS

Due to an update to the "search" system (11/23), some USPTO tutorial videos were removed and are being updated, at the time of printing this book. Review available videos BEFORE and DURING application process.

- ☐ TEAS Plus vs TEAS Standard
- ☐ Applicant Information
- ☐ Mark Drawing Page
- ☐ Additional Statements
- ☐ G & S TEAS Plus
- ☐ G & S TEAS Standard
- ☐ Filing Basis
- ☐ Correspondence Informaton
- ☐ Signature Information
- ☐ Validation Page

MENU ==> Trademarks ==> Application process ==> Apply online ==>Scroll down to Nuts & Bolts videos

and more...

TRADEMARK WORD SEARCH

Find and circle trademark related words

L	R	U	S	T	I	M	M	S	E	R	V	I	C	E	M	A	R	K	C
E	M	M	U	N	I	C	A	T	I	C	N	O	X	Y	H	G	E	7	U
G	T	I	L	I	B	9	T	A	P	L	O	C	R	E	Y	T	I	T	I
A	R	E	F	I	L	I	N	G	B	A	S	I	S	R	J	F	O	E	T
L	O	R	P	M	O	C	I	M	A	S	N	I	E	L	J	I	E	A	A
E	F	3	T	S	E	N	O	H	R	S	7	D	R	H	N	O	M	S	Y
N	A	C	U	S	T	S	U	E	P	O	R	T	V	P	E	F	R	P	S
T	X	P	I	Y	E	P	M	M	R	E	V	O	I	M	A	F	T	L	E
I	A	T	R	A	D	E	M	A	R	K	K	F	C	E	N	I	O	U	1
T	V	A	R	T	N	C	R	R	E	K	O	T	E	A	T	C	M	S	A
Y	I	T	A	C	T	I	T	I	M	M	R	T	S	A	R	E	T	I	M
P	E	C	R	E	P	M	E	R	D	N	Y	2	R	F	S	A	O	R	S
A	R	R	O	M	M	E	T	N	M	M	L	O	C	N	I	C	A	M	E
T	E	I	T	N	E	N	M	I	A	M	E	C	I	I	M	T	T	N	A
D	I	S	C	L	A	I	M	E	R	P	E	R	P	O	C	I	M	U	R
B	M	S	C	S	S	E	N	O	K	Y	T	I	L	A	P	O	R	T	C
I	S	S	C	A	R	T	S	E	M	O	G	O	O	D	S	N	O	D	H

CLASS	DISCLAIMER	FILING BASIS
GOODS	LEGAL ENTITY	MARK
OFFICE ACTION	SEARCH	SERVICE MARK
SERVICES	SPECIMEN	TAC
TEAS PLUS	TRADEMARK	1A

NOTES

Video title _____

IP PUNCH LIST™

SKETCH A LOGO OR DESIGN

IP PUNCH LIST™

PREP WORK – THE SEARCH

- ☐ *Watch USPTO tutorials

Videos/FAQ's on searching
Menu ==>
Trademarks ==>
Application Proc. =>
Search Our Trademark Database

- ☐ Do a BRAINSTORM exercise (see worksheet) to come up with 1-5 ideas for a mark, in case your idea is already registered.

- ☐ An attorney would do an extensive SEARCH. The USPTO gives YOU guidance on how to search BEFORE you apply for your mark.

- ☐ SEARCH for mark being used in commerce (as per USPTO). Use included note paper.
  - search USPTO site
  - search on social media
  - search on Google
  - search on internet

- ☐ Do a BRAINSTORM exercise (see worksheet) to determine the International Class(es) in which you want to file your mark. ==> There is a FEE per CLASS. Must select at least 1 class

- ☐ Filing basis?
  - 1(a)
  - 1(b)
  - Other (per USPTO)

- ☐ Prep your specimen

*In November 2023, the USPTO updated to a new SEARCH system. At the time of printing this book, the "TEAS Nuts and Bolts" videos were available.

Brainstorm Exercise

You may already know what word(s) you want to file for a trademark. What if the word(s), slogan, etc. is already registered? Brainstorm 1-5 new options, as you prepare to SEARCH, according to USPTO recommendations.

WORD MARK, PHRASE, ETC.

☐

WORD MARK, PHRASE, ETC.

☐

WORD MARK, PHRASE, ETC.

☐

WORD MARK, PHRASE, ETC.

☐

WORD MARK, PHRASE, ETC.

☐

SEARCH NOTES

Brainstorm Exercise

Use this worksheet to plan which International Class(es) you want to file your mark under. **There is a FEE** for each class. You must choose at least 1 of the 45 classes. Refer to the TEAS Nuts & Bolts Goods & Services video that explains the ID manual. Remember: IN USE or INTENDED USE

List goods/services IN USE or INTENDED USE
ex. socks, hoodies, combs, brushes

☐

List CLASS for each good/service
ex. 25, 21

☐

Notes

☐

Word Mark	IP PLANNER™ CARD	
		Filing basis
List goods/services		
Date First Use Anywhere: Date First Use In Commerce:		Class(es)

Word Mark	IP PLANNER™ CARD	
		Filing basis
List goods/services		
Date First Use Anywhere: Date First Use In Commerce:		Class(es)

TRADEMARK CROSSWORD PUZZLE

abandonment
branding
cease and desist
descriptive mark
examiner
fees
intent to use
likelihood of confusion
logo
registration
trademark watch
use in commerce
USPTO

ACROSS
1. Similarity could cause rejection
4. Idea of self monitoring activity
5. Section 1(b) filing basis
6. Granting of application
7. Creating an ID to goods and services
8. Symbol identifying a brand (words/design)
12. United States Patent & Trademark Office

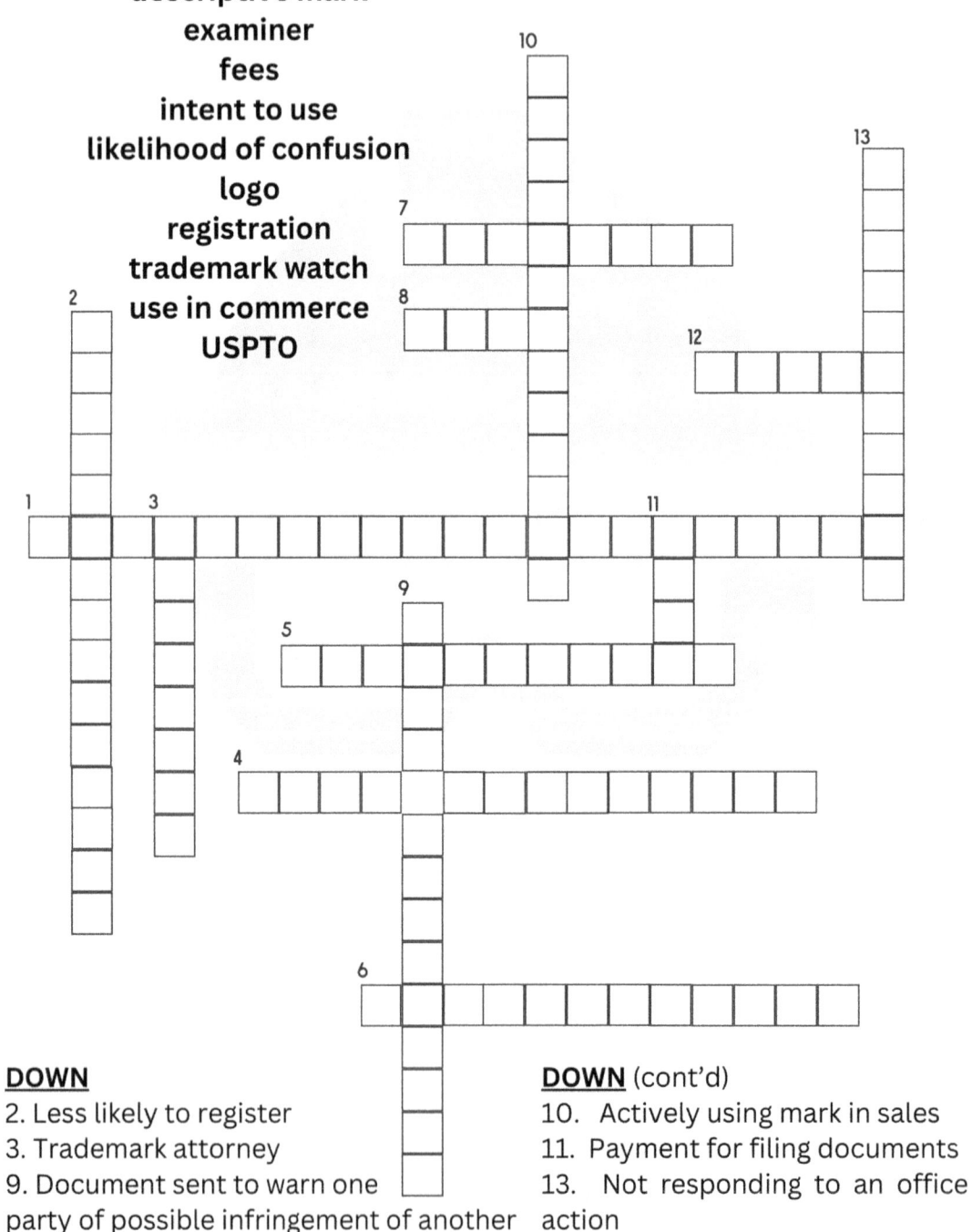

DOWN
2. Less likely to register
3. Trademark attorney
9. Document sent to warn one party of possible infringement of another

DOWN (cont'd)
10. Actively using mark in sales
11. Payment for filing documents
13. Not responding to an office action

IP PUNCH LIST ™

THE APPLICATION – YOU CAN DIY

REMEMBER: Review TEAS Nuts & Bolts videos during application process

- ☐ Go to USPTO.gov
- ☐ LOGIN with your USER ID
- ☐ MENU=>Trademarks => Appl. Process =>Apply Online
- ☐ Initial application forms- (click to proceed)
- ☐ Note: There are 5 possible application forms. The first (main) application has two filing options, TEAS plus and TEAS standard. Option 2 thru 5 (see "other initial application forms") are for **SPECIFIC** use: certification, collective, collective membership. FYI
- ☐ If option 1...
  - TEAS plus OR standard
- ☐ Specimen (jpeg)
- ☐ • 1(a) OR 1(b)

BEFORE YOU SUBMIT

- ☐ * Validation page *
- - Input (review this)
  - Mark (shows drawing)
  - Specimen (shows file)
  - Text form (look it over)
- ☐ Pay/submit
- ☐ Record serial# on IP Planner
- ☐ If you get an OFFICE ACTION, don't panic. Follow instructions on how to reply OR call help desk.
- ☐ Record registration # once reg. is granted

Reference

This book makes reference to material provided by the United States Patent and Trademark Office, at USPTO.gov.